This book belongs to

....

This book is dedicated to my mum Judy Smith
who always encouraged and loved my writing.
Thanks also to my husband Kerry and children
Caidyn and Jessica for all their love and support.
Diana

Published in Australia by
Books To Inspire Press
Perth, Western Australia
dianasmithbookstoinspire.com
author@dianasmithbookstoispire.com

First published in Australia in 2018
Text Copyright © Diana Smith 2018
Illustrations Copyright © Sarah Jane Marchant 2018

All rights reserved. No part of this publication may be reproduced, stored in a retrieval system, or transmitted, in any form or by any means without the prior written permission of the publisher, nor be otherwise circulated in any form of binding or cover other than that in which it is published and without a similar condition being imposed on the subsequent purchaser.

National Library of Australia Cataloguing in Publication entry

 A catalogue record for this book is available from the National Library of Australia

ISBN: 978-0-6489970-6-1 (paperback)
ISBN: 978-0-6452072-1-7 (hardcover)

Illustrations by Sarah Jane Marchant
Book layout and typography by Sophie White
Printed by Ingram Spark

Disclaimer: All care has been taken in the preparation of the information herein, but no responsibility can be accepted by the publisher or author for any damages resulting from the misinterpretation of this work. All contact details given in this book were current at the time of publication, but are subject to change.

My Welcome Book

DIANA SMITH

Illustrated by Sarah Jane Marchant

WELCOME to our beautiful Earth!
Today is the day of your wonderful birth.
Your JOURNEY has started,
your story is NEW,
You are very important
to those who LOVE YOU.

Every child is born with a BEAUTIFUL soul, something so SPECIAL, UNIQUE, and WHOLE.

No matter how others may treat you,
Be strong and brave,
there's nothing you can't do.

Take with you these words along the way,
you are ALWAYS good enough
every single day.

This body you have is not who you are,
It's just a tool, like driving a car.

It's your MIND that does WONDERS,
of that I am sure.

The world is such an abundant place,
From the ground at your feet
to the vastness of space.

So don't settle for small,
always DREAM BIG
Laugh and love and dance up a jig.

Make it special and joyous
and give a great cheer!

Remember to grow and learn
from your mistakes,

Listen to your heart,
and **YOU'LL
BECOME GREAT!**

www.ingramcontent.com/pod-product-compliance
Lightning Source LLC
Chambersburg PA
CBHW041429010526
44107CB00045B/1549